100 Ways to
Obtain Peace

100 Ways to Obtain Peace

Overcoming Anxiety

Richard L. Flournoy, Ph.D.
Frank B. Minirth, M.D.
Paul D. Meier, M.D.
States V. Skipper, Ph.D.

Copyright © 1985 by Baker Book House
Published by Fleming H. Revell
a division of Baker Book House Company
P.O. Box 6287, Grand Rapids, MI 49516-6287

ISBN: 0-8007-8614-9

Sixth printing, October 1996

Printed in the United States of America

All rights reserved. No part of this publication may be
reproduced, stored in a retrieval system, or transmitted in
any form or by any means—electronic, mechanical, photo-
copy, recording, or any other—without the prior written
permission of the publisher. The only exception is brief
quotations in printed reviews.

Unless otherwise indicated, all Scripture verses are from
the King James Version.

Verses marked NASB are from the New American Standard
Bible, © the Lockman Foundation 1960, 1962, 1963, 1968,
1971, 1972, 1973, 1975, 1977 and are used with permission.

Verses marked RSV are taken from the Revised Standard
Version copyrighted 1946, 1952, 1971, and 1973 by the
Division of Christian Education of the National Council of
the Churches of Christ in the United States of America and
are used with permission.

Contents

PART ONE

Relying on God
for Security

1

Trust God for Enablement

*And Moses said unto the Lord, "O my Lord, I am not eloquent,
neither heretofore, nor since thou hast spoken unto thy servant: but I
am slow of speech, and of a slow tongue." And the Lord said unto
him, "Who hath made man's mouth? or who maketh the dumb, or
deaf, or the seeing, or the blind? have not I the Lord?"*

(Exodus 4:10–11)

It is easy to become nervous, tense, and anxious when we feel that our tasks are too big for us. The truth is we all get the Moses syndrome from time to time and deny our ability to overcome the challenges that lie ahead. Our problem is not so much in underestimating ourselves as it is in underestimating God. By simply relying on God to equip us for the work he has given us, we can take the razor edge off stress.

2

Expect Supernatural Help During Trouble

Do not fear! Stand by and see the salvation of the Lord which He will accomplish for you today.

(Exodus 14:13, NASB)

These words were spoken by Moses to the Israelites moments before God miraculously parted the Red Sea. It was quite a situation. On one side of the Israelites there charged a mighty Egyptian army; on the other side there raged a fierce Red Sea. You might say they were caught between the proverbial rock and hard place. Naturally, their hearts were full of fear, and they were outraged with Moses for leading them into what appeared to be a death trap. Suddenly, supernaturally, God intervened.

At times, our fears can be very difficult to quiet. We need to learn to expect the unexpected, because so often God's rescue operation is already underway. After miraculously winning over the most exhausting circumstances, we wonder why we ever doubted God in the first place. God's ways are so unpredictable! We never know just how he's going to help us, so there's always an element of surprise. The one thing that should not surprise us is that he always does come to our aid. We can and should come to expect God's help.

3

Envision God's Invincible Protection

And when the servant of the man of God was risen early, and gone forth, behold, an host compassed the city both with horses and chariots. And his servants said unto him, "Alas, my master! how shall we do?" And he answered, "Fear not: for they that be with us are more than they that be with them." And Elisha prayed, and said, "Lord, I pray thee, open his eyes, that he may see." And the Lord opened the eyes of the young man; and he saw: and, behold, the mountain full of horses and chariots of fire round about Elisha.

(2 Kings 6:15–17)

The big edge for Christians is that God is with us. Believers caught in the grinder of life sometimes find that truth hard to imagine. In a see, smell, taste, hear, feel world invisible protection doesn't seem too invincible! So, before we become critical of this young servant, we ought to take a good look at ourselves.

Awareness of God's insurmountable hedge of protection can be a real key to emotional security. Getting mental images of how he might be shielding us from danger can go a long way toward putting our fears to rest. Try it! Then believe it is true. In fact, God's security system is far more sophisticated and elaborate than anyone can imagine. Absolutely nothing enters our lives that he does not permit.

4

Realize God's Eagerness to Help

For the eyes of the Lord run to and fro throughout the whole earth, to show himself strong in the behalf of them whose heart is perfect toward him.

(2 Chronicles 16:9a)

Anxiety is frequently caused by a fear of abandonment or a sense of loneliness. Sometimes we even erroneously fear that intimacy with God is not attainable. We fear that he won't accept us.

In this verse God announces that he is looking for people who want to know him. God longs to be close to us! People frequently feel that, in spite of their efforts, they can't get close to God. In childhood, they may have failed in their attempts to become intimate with their earthly father. As a result they wrongly transfer these same feelings of being rejected over to their heavenly Father.

This passage of Scripture shows us that, in reality, God yearns for intimacy with us and he conducts a vast, intensive search for people who need strengthening. God is eager to show us how strong he can be in our lives when our hearts (mind, emotions, and will) are completely yielded to him.

5

Trust God's Decisions in Your Life

Though he slay me, yet will I trust in him.

(Job 13:15a)

Humanly speaking, it can be incomprehensible why God allows some of the heartaches in this world, especially when the upheaval of pain visits our house.

We have three basic choices in handling trials: we can turn our anxiety inward and become depressed; we can turn anxiety outward and become angry and aggressive, inflicting hurts on others; or we can turn to God. Most people have tried the first two choices with very little success. Both of them deal crushing blows to inner peace.

On the other hand, turning to the Lord, even when we do not understand why these heartaches are happening, can initiate a relaxing calm. Sovereignty is a word for every Christian to latch on to. God is always in control. He always knows what is best, and he always does what is right. Furthermore, he is free to move as he pleases. Since his infinite mind has a total grasp of the situation, we can rest assured that he will never fail us. We can and must trust him even when we do not understand.

6

Accept God's Comfort

*The Lord is my shepherd, I shall not want; he makes me lie down in
green pastures. He leads me beside still waters; he restores my soul.
He leads me in paths of righteousness for his name's sake. Even
though I walk through the valley of the shadow of death, I fear no
evil; for thou art with me; thy rod and thy staff, they comfort me.*
(Psalm 23:1–4b, RSV)

These words have often been the source of solace
and peace. Few other biblical passages contain such beauti-
ful imagery. The reason why people are so uplifted by the
Shepherd's Psalm is because it describes the comfort we
dream of having during trials. But it doesn't have to be a
dream! It is available in Jesus Christ right this minute.

This comfort doesn't come with a mere snapping of our
fingers. We must accept God's comfort or we will not possess it. To receive this emotional healing we cannot cling to
our hurts. They must be dropped just outside the gate to
the green pastures. Then both hands and heart will be open
to receive soothing restoration of soul and spirit.

7

Believe God Will Intervene

The Lord is for me; I will not fear; What can man do to me? The Lord is for me among those who help me.

(Psalm 118:6–7a, NASB)

The anxiety-ridden person often frets and worries needlessly over matters until his or her health is threatened. God does not want that for us. The Lord knows all of us are distraught from time to time, but he does not want us to be overwhelmed or overcome by our anxieties. Underlying our thoughts, there needs to be the confidence that God will step in, even though he may not intervene when or how we had hoped. Still, upsetting fears (like financial crunches, family crises, and job conflicts) can be disconnected if only we anticipate that the Lord . . . electrify our circumstances with his power.

8

Seek Refuge in God

It is better to take refuge in the Lord than to trust in man.
(Psalm 118:8, NASB)

This is a very sad truth—sometimes people fail us. Even friends do. The saddest thing about this circumstance is that it can leave us with no one to confide in; no one to unload our troubles on. At times like these we should seek the best refuge in the universe: God himself. He is the only never-failing confidant.

9

Remember God's Constant Presence

Where can I go from Thy spirit? Or where can I flee from Thy presence? If I ascend to heaven, Thou art there; If I make my bed in Sheol, behold, Thou art there. If I take the wings of the dawn, if I dwell in the remotest part of the sea, even there Thy hand will lead me, and Thy right hand will lay hold of me.

(Psalm 139:7–10, NASB)

All of us worry about being left alone or abandoned. These are very common concerns. One of the finest promises in the Bible is: God is always with us! We never have to fear being left alone, because God is there loving us, leading us, every step of our way.

10

Meditate on God's Unconditional Love

How precious also are Thy thoughts to me, O God! How vast is the sum of them! If I should count them, they would outnumber the sand. When I awake, I am still with Thee.

(Psalm 139:17–18, NASB)

Whenever you feel insignificant (and we all certainly do at times) think about the fact that God's thoughts toward us outnumber the grains of sand on the seashore. When you woke up this morning, your loving Heavenly Father was still with you. He was there all night long thinking about you individually—loving you.

Most love in our world is given on a conditional basis. It is not unilateral. Conditional love says, "If you love me, I will love you back." At other times it says, "To the degree you love me, I will return your love."

God's love is not like that. It is very difficult for us to comprehend the depth of God's *unconditional love*. We are very significant to the almighty God who created all things, even when we erroneously, habitually, feel insignificant. We don't need to anxiously pursue acceptance through sexual prowess, materialism, power struggles, or selfish recognition. We can quit our foolish human rat race for prestige by accepting the significance God says we have in him. That will free us to devote the energy we spent in daily worrying about our importance to loving others, serving them, and accepting their love in return. That is what the abundant life (John 10:10) is all about!

11

Make a Team Effort

The horse is prepared for the day of battle, but victory belongs to the Lord.

(Proverbs 21:31, NASB)

Sometimes it is like a horse race to just squeak through another day. Facing tomorrow's second furlong can be disheartening. We question our stamina to go on.

Here's an insightful reminder: we need to be responsible and do what we can to deal with a problem ("the horse is prepared"). However that needs to be balanced with the faith that God is still in control ("victory belongs to the Lord"). No team plays two quarterbacks at the same time. Sure, take the ball and run with it. But let God call all the plays. Become a team player!

12

Depend on God's Omnipotence

"Behold, I am the Lord, the God of all flesh: is there anything too hard for me?"

(Jeremiah 32:27)

What a comfort to realize that nothing is too hard for God! If we will turn to him, he can help us overcome any problem. After all, isn't it a little difficult to imagine God being baffled? No knot is too tight for him to untie. No situation becomes impossible for him to figure out. And can you envision God saying, "Oops! I really let things get out of control down there"? Of course not. The more we depend on God's immeasurable strength the more he proves himself.

13

Rejoice that God Never Quits

God's mercies never come to an end.

(Lamentations 3:22, RSV)

Many of us have difficulty accepting that God is as generous as he is. When we repeat a failure, we have a tendency to say, "This is it. God is finished with me this time." Actually God is never finished with any of his children. You see, there is not a loophole in God's mercy.

The problem is that we take the feelings that we would have if someone wronged us and apply them to the way we wrong God. We say, "I would be finished with anyone who did that to me, so God must be finished with me." We take the feelings we have and project them onto God. Nothing could be farther from the truth. God will discipline us if we sin, because he wants us to mature. But he never "drops" us. So we can relax and enjoy God's endless mercies and thank him for his discipline. God isn't finished with us yet.

14

Get to Know the Comforter

But the Comforter, which is the Holy Ghost, whom the Father will send in my name, he shall teach you all things, and bring all things to your remembrance, whatsoever I have said unto you.

(John 14:26)

Just as a child will run to a trusted parent for comfort when hurt, we can run to God when we are hurting. More than that, God is a most loving parent and has frequently run to us when we were hurting. And how does he initiate help? Through the Comforter, the Holy Spirit. God recognizes that we have much to learn about him. The Holy Spirit is our teacher, educating us about the Lord. He also equips us to live as Christ did. It should be a great relief to know that God has provided, through the Comforter, everything we need to succeed as Christians.

15

Prove God's Thoroughness

God shall supply all your needs.

(Philippians 4:19a, NASB)

This verse is both a promise and a challenge. The promise is clear: God is a fantastic giver and he is committed to our welfare. Furthermore, he is thorough: he will provide whatever we need. By recalling this promise we can lessen our anxiety. This verse is also a challenge because it is indirectly a test of our faith. The question we must ask ourselves is, "God, can I really trust you to supply *all* my needs?"

16

Don't Fear God's Rejection

For He Himself has said, "I will never desert you, nor will I ever forsake you," so that we confidently say, "The Lord is my helper, I will not be afraid. What shall men do to me?"

(Hebrews 13:5b–6, NASB)

Nerve-racked persons intensely fear rejection by others. In fact, they feel they are nobodies and deserve rejection. Maybe the most fearful feeling they have is rejection by God. The thought that God discards people is totally unfounded. Our Lord is not a ruthless manipulator who uses people then turns his back on them. He cares deeply for his children and promises never to throw us out. What a wonderful resource of peace: with God we are always welcome!

17

Refocus Your Perspective

Let not your heart be troubled; believe in God, believe also in Me. In my Father's house are many dwelling places; if it were not so, I would have told you; for I go to prepare a place for you. And if I go and prepare a place for you, I will come again, and receive you to Myself; that where I am, there you may be also.

(John 14:1–3, NASB)

We often forfeit a peaceful existence because we have lost perspective on life. Selfishly we focus on the temporal things of this earth. But the humdrum of accumulating more things is not satisfying. In fact, it provokes dissatisfaction. Multitudes are being strangled by their entanglement in worldliness.

By dialing the focus ring on a camera we can bring a subject into clear view. Until then, things are fuzzy and blurred. Life centered on self is shadowy and indistinct, bound to be frustrating and disappointing. The truth is we need to focus our lens on Jesus, especially since this fleeting life can be filled only by him. The sharper our focus on Christ becomes, the more we will anticipate his return.

18

Trust God to Supply Needs

*Therefore do not be anxious, saying, "What shall we eat?" or
"What shall we drink?" or "What shall we wear?"*
(Matthew 6:31, RSV)

We are prone to a terrible habit: we want to be able to figure everything out and have events happen according to our plans. When things go awry, we become confused and disturbed. Whenever our needs are involved, our tendency to worry and fret increases. Instead of being crushed, we should be challenged. The challenge is to rely on Jesus to meet those needs. He promises to take care of us and provide for us. Take the challenge, and let that bad habit die. Stop figuring and start "faithing"!

PART TWO

Dealing with Negative Emotions

19

Deal with Anger Biblically

You shall not hate your fellow countryman in your heart; you may surely reprove your neighbor, but shall not incur sin because of him. You shall not take vengeance, nor bear any grudge against the sons of your people, but you shall love your neighbor as yourself; I am the Lord.

(Leviticus 19:17–18, NASB)

This verse shows that it is very appropriate for us to tactfully reprove a neighbor or friend who offends us. But we must never hold any grudges or seek vengeance. Vengeance is God's business—not ours! The unconscious motive for holding a grudge for any past offense is always vengeance, the subtle desire to "get even" with the person who angered us.

Holding grudges and a vengeful attitude are the primary root causes of depression, and both are sinful. Much anxiety comes our way when we repress our anger and are afraid to take a good look at our vengeful subconscious motives. If we would only realize that getting angry is normal and that reproving the person who offended us (before bedtime, according to Ephesians 4:26) is a godly thing to do (and even commanded), it would be much easier for us to forgive people who upset us. At the same time we might even help them change their offensive behavior.

20

Don't Give Up

*Do not be fainthearted. Do not be afraid, or panic, or tremble
before them, for the Lord your God is the one who goes with you,
to fight for you against your enemies, to save you.*

(Deuteronomy 20:3b–4, NASB)

Looking for a place to go to resign? Frustration can become a most unbearable thing. Take the Israelites, for example. This passage implies that they had had just about enough. Scared, panicky, and shaking in their boots, their physical endurance was registering empty. And then, in his timely way, God sends them a rousing message: "Don't quit!" Isn't that just like our Lord? In the middle of our most disparaging moments, he brings exactly the thing to uplift us.

That doesn't stop Satan. If he can break you down, he will. But don't give up; give in . . . to the Lord. Call out for God's strength and let him win your battles. He can change the frustrating into the fantastic before you can say, "I resign."

21

Resist Loneliness

So I will be with you; I will not fail you or forsake you.
(Joshua 1:5, RSV)

Alone. Just look at that word—such a blue-sounding word. Loneliness is a dreadful and peace-robbing emotion. It is unrealistic to think loneliness can be totally conquered once for all, but it can be resisted. We do not have to wallow in the self-pity that loneliness begs us to feel. God is with us and promises not to back out when the going gets rough. Think about it: you need never feel alone again.

22

Overcome Discouragement

And it came to pass, as they still went on, and talked, that behold, there appeared a chariot of fire, and horses of fire, and parted them both asunder; and Elijah went up by a whirlwind into heaven.

(2 Kings 2:11)

A certain mystique seems to surround Bible characters. We envision them as rugged and tough, but also tender and daring. Each day with them was a courageous adventure wherein they accomplished the unachievable and even the unbelievable. Elijah, at first glance, fits that description.

But hold everything! This prophet, who made a dramatic fiery-chariot exit from earth, had true-to-life human emotions to overcome. And discouragement was at the top of his list. Once he was so down that he prayed for God to let him die (1 Kings 19:4). Imagine that!

The amazing thing about Elijah is not his Old Testament superstardom; it is the remarkable way he overcame deep discouragement. Before his life ended he bounced back to be used of God in a bold fashion. We, too, can tackle discouragement by looking to the Lord to supply our physical, psychological, and spiritual needs. Through Christ we can ride imaginary chariots of fire everyday and face the challenges of life with a positive outlook.

23

Challenge Fear

*The Lord is my light and my salvation; whom shall I fear? The
Lord is the strong hold of my life; of whom shall I be afraid?*
(Psalm 27:1, RSV)

We are too easily buffaloed by our emotions. By
immediately giving in to the whims of our feelings, we can
quickly lose peace. And though we long for sweet peace,
there must be something in human nature that enjoys un-
leashing the dark spirit of fear within us. Millions of people
like to be frightened by horror movies or scary tales. They
relish reading anything with the element of suspense.

Fictional suspense can be entertaining and healthy. However, we must not listen to the fictional fears our emotions
so often create for us. We have a real stronghold in this life.
Thank God, when we're too weak to hang on tight, he never
lets go.

24

Experience Sublime Security

Because you have made the Lord your refuge, the Most High your habitation, no evil shall befall you, no scourge come near your tent. For he will give his angels charge of you to guard you in all your ways.

(Psalm 91:9–11, RSV)

The anxious nonbeliever has no refuge, no real peace. But the believer, even when anxious, does have refuge. Believers can find genuine peace because God is our refuge. God has promised us security when we come running to Him. While both believers and nonbelievers may suffer from anxiety, only believers can rest secure. They know that God grants us freedom from the strains of carrying our burdens alone. He carries our burdens for us. In fact, many times he carries us.

25

Meditate on Your Significance to God

O Lord, Thou hast searched me and known me. Thou dost know when I sit down and when I rise up; Thou dost understand my thought from afar. Thou dost scrutinize my path and my lying down, and art intimately acquainted with all my ways. Even before there is a word on my tongue, behold, O Lord, Thou dost know it all. Thou hast enclosed me behind and before, and laid Thy hand upon me. Such knowledge is too wonderful for me; it is too high, I cannot attain to it.

(Psalm 139:1–6, NASB)

Do you ever wince back pains of feeling unloved and insignificant? If so, then examine the principle that underlies this psalm: God is infinitely interested in you and also in the puniest details of your life; you are immeasurably loved by him. That truth is just too wonderful to comprehend! In fact, the mysteries of it are enough to melt down a home computer programmed to find the answer why. There is no why.

God's love is unconditional; we do not have to perform nor provide in order to be the objects of his care. He knows our unspoken thoughts and desires, and evil though they be, loves us everlastingly. That is something very much worth meditating on.

26

Keep Your Inner Light Shining

If I say, "Surely the darkness will overwhelm me, and the light around me will be night," even the darkness is not dark to Thee, and the night is as bright as the day. Darkness and light are alike to Thee.

(Psalm 139:11–12, NASB)

The insomniacs of America club is one of the largest nonmembership groups in this country. Several million Americans pay their dues secretly every night when they turn out the lights and pull up the covers. The darkness is louder than thunder, and sleep is ever so slow in coming. The darkness gets louder and seems to cry out. The whole process is agonizing.

If this is happening to you, what you need is a night light. Actually, it's more like an inner light, one that says, "I can rest assured, with God there is no night!" Before you know it, the next thing you see will be tomorrow's sunshine.

27

Don't Worry About Incorrectable "Defects"

For Thou didst form my inward parts; Thou didst weave me in my mother's womb. I will give thanks to Thee, for I am fearfully and wonderfully made; wonderful are Thy works, and my soul knows it very well. My frame was not hidden from Thee, when I was made in secret, and skillfully wrought in the depths of the earth. Thine eyes have seen my unformed substance; and in Thy book they were all written, the days that were ordained for me, when as yet there was not one of them.

(Psalm 139:13–16, NASB)

Are you distressed over incorrectable "defects" in your mind or body? Do you wish you had a higher IQ? Do you have a genetic disease or defect? Do you wish you were shorter, taller, or just arranged differently?

Sometimes, in our desire to be perfect in every way, we forget that the unchangeable characteristics we possess were designed by God. None of us are the perfect specimen of humankind. The Lord gave each of us some strengths and some weaknesses. Furthermore, he can use both our high points and our low points to bring glory to his name.

Rather than wasting our emotional energy worrying about the weaknesses or defects that cannot be removed, we should concentrate on allowing God the freedom to work in our lives as he sees fit.

28

Expose Your Unconscious Thoughts

Search me, O God, and know my heart; Try me and know my anxious thoughts; And see if there be any hurtful way in me, And lead me in the everlasting way.

(Psalm 139:23–24, NASB)

What an insightful idea—Let God uncover your innermost thoughts! In some cases, lodged beneath the surface of our emotions is a harmful pattern of behavior. Things are noticeably wrong with our actions, but we can't pinpoint why. Underneath lies the answer. Some unconscious thought is embedded in the heart. Since it is the heart that often motivates us (heart = mind + emotions + will), whenever it is affected by murky reasoning we usually walk in the "hurtful way," instead of in the "everlasting way." By praying for God to floodlight our deepest feelings with his guidance, we can be returned to the right road—which is also the road of serenity! With God transparency is the best policy!

29

Reject Worrying as a Solution

And which of you by being anxious can add a cubit to his span of life? If then you are not able to do as small a thing as that, why are you anxious about the rest?

(Luke 12:25–26, RSV)

Thousands of words have been written and spoken about the absurdity of worrying. Already many of you are nodding in agreement. And what's more, you have conceded that this is something you need to hear again. Let's try to look at it in a different light this time.

Somehow, we have convinced ourselves that by worrying hard enough we will find a solution. But we will not. In fact, most of our fretting is over something that doesn't even exist, much less need solving. The truth is, we like clutching our worries tightly to ourselves. We hold them snugly and smugly, because we suppose they give us comfort. Finally, however, they exasperate us, beginning a whole new dreaded cycle of worrying.

Mark worry for what it is—self-centeredness! Since it offers no solutions, expect none from it. Look to Christ instead.

30

Clear Up Confusion

For God is not a God of confusion but of peace.
(1 Corinthians 14:33, RSV)

 S ome days life amazes us, other days it just "mazes" us. Plainly, it can get very confusing. We find ourselves shrouded with doubt and unclear about what to do next. Fast on the heels of bewilderment is tension, another popular peace thief. God is the only one who can evaporate our foggy perspective and replace the tension with twinkle, the gleam of spiritual visibility.

31

Prevent Bitterness from Growing

Let all bitterness, and wrath, and anger, and clamor, and evil
speaking, be put away from you, with all malice.

(Ephesians 4:31)

Bitterness is never satisfied to stay small. It is never happy being a tiny grudge. Out of grudges bitterness feeds and grows. Ignoring it, or pretending it is not there, makes for some deep roots of bitterness. While they grow under the surface for a time, one day they will sprout into a destructive tree of wrath. In the meantime, peace is long gone and so is good mental health. Nip bitterness in the bud; seek forgiveness instinctively, and dole it out lavishly. Sweet ground rarely produces bitter fruit.

PART THREE

Applying Insight
to Living

32

Learn from God's Testings

Do not be afraid; for God has come in order to test you, and in order that the fear of Him may remain with you, so that you may not sin.
(Exodus 20:20, NASB)

Moses made this statement. We can apply this verse to our daily lives by refusing to allow Satan to upset us with paranoid fears concerning God. God is not our enemy and we do not need to be scared of him, in a negative sense.

Still, remember that God does allow stressful situations to develop in our lives in order to test or "check out" our faith. Spiritual exams of our faith in God can be of much help. They can help us get our priorities straight. They can give us insight into personal changes that we need to make in our relationships with God and others. God's testing will encourage and remind us to respect and reverence God and his Word. Consequently we will discipline our lives so that we can grow in the faith and knowledge of God, and thereby avoid sin.

33

Yield the Controls to God

Agree with God, and be at peace; thereby good will come to you.
(Job 22:21, RSV)

Arguing with God is the most preposterous thing a human can do. Of course, you and I would never do such a thing. Or would we? The truth is that we like to be in charge of the control panels of our lives. We don't want God pushing any buttons that could jeopardize the plans we have made. God is relegated to backseat driving, because he causes us a lot less interference back there. Naturally, though, after we crash we expect a full explanation from God as to why he let it happen. His answer is the same as always: "Leave the driving to me!" In other words, agree with God today that from now on you will let him be in complete control.

34

Meditate Your Way to Peace

But his delight is in the law of the Lord; and in his law doth he meditate day and night. And he shall be like a tree planted by the rivers of water, that bringeth forth his fruit in his season; his leaf also shall not wither; and whatsoever he doeth shall prosper.

(Psalm 1:2–3)

Here's a word that doesn't get enough ink: *meditate*. Maybe the strange rituals of Eastern religions have made us leery or suspicious of this practice. That's understandable. However, total neglect of this lost art can leave us spiritually lopsided. Meditation is peace and quiet par excellence.

Biblical meditation doesn't require candle-lighting ceremonies and yoga positions on oriental rugs. It is a matter of allowing Scripture to flood the mind, letting it cascade like a waterfall through the thoughts, until each sparkling droplet ripples into a shimmering, placid oasis for the soul. It is the purest form of escapism around. And it is quite legal, even recommended, because it gives us insight into the truest aspects of reality.

35

Practice Resting

Rest in the Lord and wait patiently for Him.

(Psalm 37:7, NASB)

We don't get enough rest—spiritual rest, that is. The routine panic in which many of us live daily is indicative of the inner merry-go-round that spins even faster. Whenever pressure points come (like surgery, new career moves, test scores, emergencies, and tragedies) we churn away on the inside like an electric ice-cream maker.

It's hard work to learn how to rest properly. We believe we are remiss to just sit quietly at the feet of Jesus. Like Martha we think we should be busy, busy, busy. And we can't relate to the Marys of the world who are able to sit still when there are so many things to be done (or worried about).

Resting spiritually is not laziness. It does not mean shirking responsibility. It is the calm assurance that God is working right on schedule.

36

Acquire and Exercise Wisdom

My son, let them not depart from your sight; Keep sound wisdom and discretion, so they will be life to your soul, and adornment to your neck. Then you will walk in your way securely, and your foot will not stumble. When you lie down, you will not be afraid; When you lie down, your sleep will be sweet.

(Proverbs 3:21–24, NASB)

Wisdom remains a cherished, but rare, commodity. The scarcity of it is largely due to the fact that so few people know anything about it. This crowning jewel of character traits is solely God-given, although it cannot be received without a reverential adventure into the worship of God himself. Even then, wisdom seems to come in installments which accrue benefits whenever it is exercised.

The practical use of God-given insight can bring security, stability, and satisfying sleep: the antithesis of anxiety. That makes wisdom another link in the blueprint of peace. Find and use this priceless treasure!

37

Sow Encouragement

Heaviness in the heart of man maketh it stoop but a good word maketh it glad.

(Proverbs 12:25)

Tension, hyperalertness, irritability, worrying, poor sleep, perspiration, headaches, hyperventilation, nervous stomach, rapid heart beat, urinary frequency, impotence, and frigidity—these are the symptoms of anxiety. Anxiety causes not only physical disorders but also the majority of mental disorders. Put the blame where it belongs: squarely on the shoulders of anxiety. That is exactly what scripture means about heaviness.

The prescription to heal anxiety is encouragement. If the law of sowing and reaping is still in effect (and it is), then one can expect to receive in return whatever is planted. Encourage others and reap the fruits that kindness bears. Furthermore, you will reap encouragement from others who appreciate the considerate way you have ministered to them. Suddenly, the symptoms are forgotten.

38

Respond to Spiritual Conviction

The sinners in Zion are afraid; trembling has seized the godless.
(Isaiah 33:14, RSV)

There is a healthy fear—the fear or reverential awe of God. Whenever Christians allow their lifestyles to follow carnal appetites, the ensuing pressure from guilt in the conscience is part of God's unique alarm system to the soul. Disregarding the warning he sends through spiritual conviction is certain to unleash even greater tension, leading ultimately to an absolute loss of peace.

On the other hand, obeying the promptings of God's Spirit produces freedom. The heavy weight so quickly caused by sin evaporates.

Being ensnared in the anxiety-ridden chains of sin is not the party it is cracked up to be. When the chains are broken by the love of God's forgiveness, the celebration really begins!

39

Begin Using Your Faith

Why are ye fearful, O ye of little faith?

(Matthew 8:26)

Did you catch the implication of this verse? Fear comes from sickly faith. To be blunt, it is the result of not being "gutsy" enough to exercise however much faith already exists in us. Our problem isn't the amount of our faith; it's not using the faith we have.

Jesus said mustard seed-sized faith is enough to do the impossible. That is, if it is operative. Then again, if it isn't alive it isn't really faith. We wish and dream a lot, which hasn't moved a mountain yet. But when someone believes—truly believes—and acts on it, apprehension vanishes and victory results! Try using the faith you have instead of looking for more.

The strange thing about hard-working faith is that it reproduces itself!

40

Peace Is a Choice

Peace I leave with you; My peace I give to you; not as the world gives, do I give to you. Let not your heart be troubled, nor let it be fearful.

(John 14:27, NASB)

God's marvelous peace is available this very moment, but to have it you must make a conscious, mental choice to possess it. The feelings of sadness, helplessness, hopelessness, worthlessness, and loneliness are also choices. Unfortunately, they appear to be the more popular choices today.

Don't misunderstand. Peace cannot be obtained as simply as saying, "Well, I'm just not going to be sad any more. I'm going to be at peace." No, that kind of oversimplification only magnifies frustration. Peace eludes us until we make a solid choice to have it. And yet, few actually make this uncompromising choice.

This ulcerated world has learned to stomach heartache and turmoil, by doling out its own quick-fix medicine labeled "peace." But no lasting peace ever comes. Nonetheless, the world's peace remains the choice of the masses—empty, vain living.

An alternative is available to cure the deep ills of the human heart. It is the peace God gives when we choose to live life as prescribed by the Great Physician.

41

Hold On to Hope

We are troubled on every side, yet not distressed; we are perplexed, but not in despair; Persecuted, but not forsaken; cast down, but not destroyed.

(2 Corinthians 4:8–9)

Knocked down but not knocked out—that's how someone once described the situation described in these verses. Hope grows dim very fast when the strange twists of life throw their knock-out punches. After being badly beaten by pain or grief or loss, who cares about hope anyway? Who is excited about beginning again? Answer: almost nobody.

Like a boxer who has taken eleven rounds of pummeling, that last fall to the canvas feels good in a way—good enough to keep a dizzy man down. Fighting four more rounds loses its luster. But why does he want so badly to get up? Answer: he still hopes to win.

The hope promised to God's children is not like wishing; there is nothing uncertain about our hope. If we hold our hope tightly, the victory is already ours. All we have to do is stay in the fight. And who throws the final knockout blow? Answer: God does.

42

Express Positive Concern

For I have no one else of kindred spirit who will genuinely be concerned for your welfare.

(Philippians 2:20, NASB)

The Greek word we translate as anxiety is interpreted in this verse as the word *concerned*. It is obviously used in a positive sense here. In fact, approximately five out of the twenty-five times that the word is used in the Greek New Testament, it is used in a positive sense. When used in this positive sense, it connotes a realistic concern.

In other words, anxiety in the form of a realistic concern is healthy. It is not healthy when it denotes fretting or worrying, as it does in Philippians 4:6 ("Be anxious for nothing").

Psychological research has shown the same distinction to be true. With a little anxiety (realistic concern) employees are more efficient. With a little anxiety, recovery from surgery is better than when there was either no or intense preoperative apprehension.

The concept is stated well in 2 Corinthians 4:8–9: "We are afflicted in every way, but not crushed; perplexed, but not despairing; persecuted, but not forsaken; struck down but not destroyed." Naturally, the apostle Paul had a realistic concern in such circumstances, but because of Jesus, he was not "crushed." We can identify with this truth today. We can also look at life through the eyes of realism, displaying a genuine concern true to our humanity but not detrimental to our spirituality.

43

Be Content

But godliness with contentment is great gain.

(1 Timothy 6:6)

Contentment is a rare possession today, it seems. Here the apostle Paul was encouraging Timothy to be content in regard to material things. What a good lesson that is for us. A cancer of anxiety spreads without such contentment.

Contentment also can involve many areas of our lives and give peace from stress. Maybe you have seen the pithy saying, "All I will ever want is a little more than I will ever have." What a jarring reminder that we are prone to dissatisfaction, as well as ingratitude, for the things we presently possess! By keeping a handy list of the wonderful blessings we have to be thankful for (like health, job, friends, family, salvation, country, and material possessions), we have at our fingertips a valuable tool to shape our contentment. Of course, the list has to be a sincere reflection of our heart attitude. Otherwise, it isn't worth the paper it is written on.

By practicing true contentment we can change that little saying to: "All I will ever have is more than I will ever want."

44

Acquire Grace and Mercy

Grace, mercy, and peace from God the Father and Christ Jesus our Lord.

(2 Timothy 1:2, NASB)

Meet the sisters of peace: Grace and Mercy. The first is the ability to give to others that which they do not deserve; the second is the ability to withhold from others that reproof which they do deserve. When these qualities are interwoven in our living, the end result will be peace.

God is the only one who has the absolute control of grace and mercy because they are inherent in his character. In fact, these two gems are beyond our human capabilities. If we are to be equipped to demonstrate exclusively God-like characteristics, then we must be endowed by God.

Scripture says God gives more grace to the humble (John 4:6), and that mercy can be obtained through prayer (Heb. 4:16). So then, by reverently seeking the Lord in prayer we can acquire grace and mercy to help us in our time of need. In turn, we will be able to show grace and mercy unto others. Always on the heels of the first two sisters is the third sister—Peace.

45

Allow Patience to Grow

My brethren, count it all joy when ye fall into divers temptations;
Knowing this, that the trying of your faith worketh patience. But let
patience have her perfect work, that ye may be perfect and entire,
wanting nothing.

(James 1:2–4)

Trials can produce anxiety or, as stated here, patience. Trials can either destroy us or help us. In other words, trials can establish our faith, and our faith is compared to gold. However, as valuable as gold is, faith is said to be "more precious" because it does not perish.

Recognizing that God can use trials to bolster patience in us is perhaps the best handle to grasping the whys of any predicament. If we can learn to step back for a moment and evaluate the situation, we might soon see that God is doing a work in us. It won't remove the difficulty of the circumstances, but it will light a spark of joy within. Allowing patience to grow deep roots through the process of trials will not only make life more peaceful, but it will also make us better persons afterward.

46

Eliminate Hypocrisy

But the wisdom from above is first pure, then peaceable, gentle, reasonable, full of mercy and good fruits, unwavering, without hypocrisy. And the seed whose fruit is righteousness is sown in peace by those who make peace.

(James 3:17–18, NASB)

Our word *hypocrite* originated as a stage term for classical Greek actors. A hypocrite in ancient Greece would play one role wearing a certain appropriate mask. He would then dash off stage and change masks, returning to play an entirely different role. It was a unique acting form.

Today's hypocrite isn't so rare. But real life hypocrisy has its price tag. The tension created by trying to be two separate characters is counter-productive to peace. Genuineness is the trait that liberates us from play-acting.

47

Apply Suffering Wisely

But the God of all grace, who hath called us unto his eternal glory by Christ Jesus, after that ye have suffered a while, make you perfect, stablish, strengthen, settle you.

(1 Peter 5:10)

Suffering is different from carrying our cross daily. Bearing a cross is a mark of discipleship, and a test of submission. Suffering is the consequence of being faithful to the cross we carry. Certain agonies accompany the journey to Christlikeness, and they cannot be avoided.

However, suffering need not diminish the comfort we know in our Lord. As a matter of fact, suffering may deepen our intimacy with Christ, in that he suffered greatly.

It is virtually impossible to list the valuable lessons taught in the classroom of suffering. Nonetheless, not among the least is a new insight into the pain of others. This expands our usefulness, enhancing our self-worth, giving us that good feeling we so often associate with peace.

48

Search Out Perfect Love

There is no fear in love; but perfect love casts out fear.
(1 John 4:18, NASB)

Notice that perfect (complete) love casts out fear. God is the only resource of this kind of love. This is a unilateral, unconditional love that says, "I will love you regardless of what you are able to return to me." Out of such love emerges an unselfish self, one that demonstrates loving concern instead of despairing of life's crisis.

PART FOUR

Finding Encouragement
Through Relationships

49

Speak Gently

A gentle answer turns away wrath, but a harsh word stirs up anger.
(Proverbs 15:1, NASB)

Often at the heart of inner conflict are tense situations with others. And let's face it, tense situations are almost unavoidable at times. We do not say this in a condoning fashion. The sin nature being what it is, and we being weak as we are at times, and Satan being a subtle tempter, we are sometimes trapped into angry confrontations.

God has a solution: speak softly and carry no stick. His ideal is that we respond gently to those who arouse the meanest aspects of our flawed nature. When we would most like to scream back in our own defense, God offers a better way, a way to peace. Why? Because he knows that as the decibels go up, so does the blood pressure. Our physical health takes a beating; our emotional well-being suffers a nerve-racking fit, at least; and our spiritual strength is drained dry.

A gentle reply isn't easy. As a matter of fact, it is humanly impossible to consistently react with gentleness. Ask for God's help in quieting your voice. Then others will find you difficult to argue with. They may even be moved to consider your viewpoint.

50

Forgive Offenses

A man's discretion makes him slow to anger, and it is his glory to overlook a transgression.

(Proverbs 19:11, NASB)

I'll forgive it, but I won't forget it!" is just another way to say, "No, I really don't forgive you." Holding grudges certainly will not feed peace. Rather, we should be so at ease in Christ that intimidating us into anger is hard to do. Too many anxiety buffs are dominated by a spirit that jumps at the chance to get even.

We are not meant to be doormats; neither are we defenseless under the abusiveness of hate-filled people. In circumstances where it is imperative that we stand up for God's honor in our lives, Scripture does not forbid us to do so. However, we are not allowed to explode through life with a short fuse. Whatever the injustice we may suffer, God tells us to forgive it, so that we can be freed from the shackles of anger.

51

Develop Friendships

Two are better than one; because they have a good reward for their labor. For if they fall, the one will lift up his fellow: but woe to him that is alone when he falleth; for he hath not another to help him up.

(Ecclesiastes 4:9–10)

Friends offer protection against anxiety. If we are alone in our battles, it is not a matter of if we fall but only when. God desires that we have a strong support system. Then we can lift each other up when we fall. Do you have a good Christian friend to confide in, who will give you Bible-centered advice to lift you up?

52

Return Friendship

Again, if two lie together, then they have heat: But how can one be warm alone? And if one prevail against him, two shall withstand him: and a threefold cord is not quickly broken.

(Ecclesiastes 4:11–12)

Just as peace-building as having a dependable friend is being one. It will bring you a special feeling to be so highly regarded by someone that you are his/her confidant. Returning friendship—establishing harmony in sharing—can be very rewarding. At night, when you flip out the lights to go to sleep, it will be gratifying to know that your godly friendship uplifted someone who not so long ago gave you an ear and a tender heart. You'll sleep better.

53

Build Up the Broken

Say to those who are of a fearful heart, "*Be strong, fear not!*"
(Isaiah 35:4, RSV)

Positive words almost always have a confidence-building effect. This does not mean flattery, mind you. It is the knack of timely encouragement directed at healing the damaged emotions of others. Such a calming atmosphere flows from this kind of mending that it is absorbed by the encourager as much as by the broken one.

54

Communicate Freely

Do not be anxious beforehand about what you are to say, but say whatever is given you in that hour; for it is not you who speaks, but it is the Holy Spirit.

(Mark 13:11, NASB)

For some people, it is extremely taxing to verbalize problems and conflicts. The whole idea of opening up in discussion is terrorizing. What's more, the people with this fear dislike their inability to put their feelings into words. And yet, put them on the spot and the "jitters" will breed "butterflies." This nervousness about communicating creeps over into other areas of life and endangers smooth, healthy, peaceful relationships. By yielding our thoughts and words to the Holy Spirit we can be assured of divine guidance in speaking our peace—if you catch the play on words.

55

Live Peaceably

Finally, brethren, rejoice, and be made complete, be comforted, be like-minded, live in peace; and the God of love and peace shall be with you.

(2 Corinthians 13:11, NASB)

As professional counselors, we often meet people who, for various reasons, have rejected the give-and-take of Christian fellowship. They hold grudges, refuse to open honest communications, and are quick to criticize. They have chosen to be superficial in relationships. Sheltering themselves from meaningful friendships, they escape the risk of being hurt but run the risk of being all alone. Some people find themselves alone because they simply haven't learned how to get along with others. They don't know how to be open. Years of grudge-holding and closed communication have left them unable to build peaceable fellowship with others. Our verse offers God's perfect advice—harmonize! Birds of a feather (Christians) should flock together.

56

Keep a Proper Perspective on Burdens

Bear ye one another's burdens, and so fulfill the law of Christ. . . .
For every man shall bear his own burden.

(Galatians 6:2–5)

These two verses, both in the same paragraph, seem outwardly to contradict each other, but God's Word has no contradictions. In this passage, the apostle Paul is teaching each person to carry his own *normal emotional load* ("bear his own burden"), but to be lovingly available to help brothers and sisters with *temporary emotional overloads* ("one another's burdens"). Sometimes we, as believers, err by taking on a person's normal emotional burden as our own, thus accidentally encouraging irresponsibility in them, as well as short-circuiting ourselves. We do dependent persons a favor by refusing to take on their normal loads as our own concern. On the other hand, we fulfill the law of Christ when we lovingly do what we can to help each other through temporary emotional "overloads."

57

Resolve Problems Readily

Therefore, laying aside falsehood, speak truth, each one of you,
with his neighbor, for we are members of one another. Be angry,
and yet do not sin; do not let the sun go down on your anger, and
do not give the devil an opportunity.

(Ephesians 4:25–27, NASB)

Do you believe that some anger is normal? Well, some anger is normal, However, most of our indignant feelings revolve around our own petty wounds. Anger, in these cases, is unjustified and sinful.

At other times, when we suffer a significant loss or someone sins against us, then irritation is automatic and normal. But here is where a good deal of people make a vital mistake; they brood over these injustices until their anger overtakes them. They do not resolve these encroachments quickly enough.

Anger is not something to sleep on. Like a splinter, it festers. At first it is barely noticed. But soon it is swollen and painful. Most dreadful of all is finally having to get it out in the open. This festering process is so unfortunate, because the healing could have begun much sooner had the irritation been removed immediately. Start a no-after-bedtime anger policy today. You'll dream better!

58

Need and Be Needed

Is anyone among you suffering? Let him pray. Is anyone cheerful?
Let him sing praises. Is anyone among you sick? Let him call for
the elders of the church, and let them pray over him.

(James 5:13–14, NASB)

When times of trials or suffering come, God does not expect us to pretend they do not exist. He knows we need comfort during these times. Besides offering shelter beneath his own wings, God also points us in the direction of the family of believers to lift us up. We are urged to share our anxious experiences with those who will give us their prayer support. Of course, this sharing should never be done in a self-piteous way to manipulate attention. Rather, it should be a straightforward, honest sharing in hopes of informing fellow Christians who practice praying for others. In like turn, it is only right that we allow ourselves to be needed by others who are facing difficulties. Learning to sing and pray with fellow believers during low tides is the key to a secret aspect of peace—unity!

59

Try Accountability Friendship

Therefore, confess your sins to one another, and pray for one another, so that you may be healed.

(James 5:16, NASB)

A big part of living the Christian life is helping others and allowing others to help us. As we confess to one another and pray for each other, we find a new strength we did not know before. With a brother or sister in Christ we can confess not only our sins but also our worries, our anxieties, our fears, our doubts, and any burden we have. Confession is good for our mental health and spiritual well-being because it relieves the burdens and allows Christ Jesus to enter our lives and change us according to his will. It produces an accountability factor that acts as a preventative measure to repeating peace-destructive sins and habits.

PART FIVE

Avoiding
Damaging Obstacles

60

Confront Anxiety

I am weary with my groaning; all the night make I my bed to swim; I water my couch with my tears. Mine eye is consumed because of grief; it waxeth old because of all mine enemies.

(Psalm 6:6–7)

Sometimes anxiety becomes almost unbearable. If normal measures have been taken to relieve unusual tension and yet it persists, then seeing a qualified Christian counselor might be the next step. One way to begin is by having a private conversation with a pastor.

Whatever the case may be, it is unwise to allow anxiety to build and gather strength. It must be confronted . . . the sooner the better. Even King David needed the rebuke and advice of Nathan the prophet. Avoiding such necessary help for long is bound to result in further damage to the emotions and nerves. If anxiety has gotten out of hand, pray for God to provide the proper Christian counselor. The problem can be attacked and solved with qualified help.

61

Put Away Your Fear

Though a host encamp against me, my heart will not fear; though war arise against me, in spite of this I shall be confident.
(Psalm 27:3, NASB)

It is simple-minded to think we can be forever rid of all our fears. As a matter of fact, some fear is a healthy, God-given response to danger. However, when we clutch our fears and dwell on them, this is unhealthy.

Carrying fears like a "security blanket" is detrimental to peace. But here is an amazing observation: some people do not want to let go of their fears. In a strange sort of way they enjoy the attention they receive from others when they remain fearful. What they do not realize is that peace of mind continues to elude them. Only by putting away growing apprehension can one escape total slavery to fear. Once freed from the chains of trepidation, the joys of confident peace can gallop through the soul.

62

Overcome Passivity

When I kept silence, my bones waxed old through my roaring all the day long. For day and night thy hand was heavy upon me: my moisture is turned into the drought of summer. I acknowledged my sin unto thee, and mine iniquity have I not hid. I said, I will confess my transgressions unto the Lord; and thou forgavest the iniquity of my sin.

(Psalm 32:3–5)

Being passive toward difficulties will not produce tranquility, rather, it will build walls. These walls are better known as unhealthy defense mechanisms. We use these little tricks to protect ourselves from hurts, but they only stave off reality. This prolongs the slough of discouragement in our lives, slowing us down from reaching out for forgiveness.

Here are a few of the defense mechanisms we use subconsciously to cope with wrong in a passive way:

Rationalization—avoiding the supernatural by using human reasoning

Projection—blaming others for our problems

Somatization—lethargically hiding from reality by sleeping and being indifferent and sluggish

Phariseeism—relying upon inflexible rules to govern all of life

Suppression—ignoring the existence of difficulties

Confession is God's way. Be assertive instead of passive, and seek God's forgiveness by confessing the sins that have accumulated and been bottled up inwardly. Then forgive yourself on the grounds that God has forgiven you. This is the only way to knock down the wall between you and serenity.

63

Look Out for Despair

I sought the Lord, and He answered me, And delivered me from all my fears.

(Psalm 34:4, NASB)

Have you ever reached the place where you thought that God didn't care about you and wasn't listening to your prayers? This is what despair is all about—getting so emotionally low that you become dominated by frustration.

Those caught in this net find that the untangling isn't easy. These victims usually tie themselves into tighter knots by thrashing around in their own anger and self-pity. If you feel trapped in a web of despair, then do the thing that you want to do the least: pray! For no matter how much confidence you have lost in prayer, it brings one of the sweetest forms of relief: heavenly amity.

64

Reject Escapism

Fear and trembling come upon me; and horror has overwhelmed me. And I said, "O that I had wings like a dove! I would fly away and be at rest."

(Psalm 55:5–6, NASB)

Ever felt like going AWOL? Like running away from everything and starting a whole new life in a different place? It is tempting to want to get away from the events that seem to overwhelm us, but rarely does anyone who performs a Houdini act on life really get away. There is a fresh set of pitfalls in the terrain of the greener grass on the other side of the fence.

It is much better to face life's trials and grow through them. God has certain lessons for each of us to learn, and they are inescapable. By accepting these challenges we become better persons, equipped with the tools for wiser living.

65

Beware of Intense Temptation

But he that sinneth against me wrongeth his own soul.
(Proverbs 8:36a)

Satan is the master tempter. He will employ every evil device he can to ensnare you. Anxiety is no stranger to his bag of tricks. When personal pressure increases, expect him to tighten his screws, too. During these times he will make sinful actions look more appealing than ever before. Resist him and he will flee from you. Sin is temporary relief. Lasting relief comes from God.

66

Shun Alcoholic Beverages

Wine is a mocker, strong drink a brawler, And whoever is intoxicated by it is not wise.

(Proverbs 20:1, NASB)

There are over 14 million people in America today who are alcoholics and have turned to alcohol to cope with their anxieties. The answer to our problem is not to turn to alcohol but to God. People who use alcohol to kill their emotional pain or to raise their low spirits are gradually sinking lower into despondency. The Lord Jesus Christ is the best salve for the emotions. He is the Balm of Gilead. Exchange the bottle for the Book. Let the ointment of God's Word heal your soul.

67

Put Money into Perspective

And the seed which fell among the thorns, these are the ones who have heard, and as they go on their way they are choked with worries and riches and pleasures of this life, and bring no fruit to maturity.

(Luke 8:14, NASB)

Concentrating on the "almighty dollar" is a good way to tighten the noose of worry around your neck. Some people are choking peacefulness right out of their lives by making money their number-one motivation for survival. They have no time to enjoy life because they are too busy making a living.

Money is a base part of our existence; it pays for necessities and luxuries. However, money is not life. Since one does not have to own much to have the peace of God, money should be relegated to a low position on the totem pole of life.

68

Prepare to Resist

There hath no temptation taken you but such as is common to man: but God is faithful, who will not suffer you to be tempted above that ye are able; but will with the temptation also make a way to escape, that ye may be able to bear it.

(1 Corinthians 10:13)

Whenever a Christian is trekking smoothly in life, Satan will induce pressure with various temptations. The stronger the believer, the stronger the temptation. The continuous agony of satanic persistence can become an obstacle to calmness of soul.

Repeated resistance and victory, coupled with scripture memorization, can develop keen spiritual sinews. The more you exercise God's power during temptations—becoming indefatigable—the less Satan's attacks will affect your peaceful attitude of heart. But do not expect that he will give up nor miss his chance to destroy you in your weakest moment.

Since life is a spiritual war, how obvious it should be that we need a vital relationship with Christ in order to not only merely survive but also to live abundantly.

69

Age Gracefully

For while we are still in this tent, we sigh with anxiety; not that we would be unclothed, but that we would be further clothed, so that what is mortal may be swallowed up by life. He who has prepared us for this very thing is God, who has given us the Spirit as a guarantee.

(2 Corinthians 5:4–5, RSV)

Some things about growing older are not very attractive: health problems increase, the wear and tear of life takes its toll, and little aggravations multiply. Nonetheless, it is quite possible to age with beauty—a beauty of spirit, that is. Those who accept the changes of middle and later life gracefully are both an inspiration and a joy to be around.

Someday God will give all believers a glorious body that never grows old. Until then, you're only as old as you feel. It's a matter of attitude and spirit.

70

Don't Dwell on Past Mistakes

Therefore, if anyone be in Christ, he is a new creature. Old things are passed away; behold all things are become new.

(2 Corinthians 5:17)

Fretting over past blunders robs many people of happy living. Their extremely sensitive consciences still feel guilty and often they do not allow themselves growing room. It is characteristic for them to seek forgiveness numerous times for an action that happened several months or years ago.

However, our verse presents a point for the conscience-sensitive to consider. The word *become* in the original Greek implies present tense with continuing action. So a better rendering might read: all things are becoming new.

God gives us a new life in Christ; that's absolute forgiveness! Then he daily chips away at the flaws in our character and personality. We are his craftsmanship displaying his handiwork. Past blemishes that he removed long ago through forgiveness should not be painfully recalled because of hypersensitivity. We should concentrate, rather, on the rough edges that need to be sandpapered off today.

71

Stay Single-Minded

Submit yourselves therefore to God. Resist the devil, and he will flee from you. Draw nigh to God, and he will draw nigh to you. Cleanse your hands, ye sinners; and purify your hearts, ye double minded.

(James 4:7–8)

Have you noticed that it is popular with some Christians to blame the devil for their own sinful, irresponsible behavior? This temporarily relieves the guilt feelings that harass them. While the devil is certainly on the warpath to harm us, he does not have the power to possess believers ("Greater is he that is in you, than he that is in the world," 1 John 4:4).

It is the double-minded, dual-purposed Christians who suffer satanic oppression. The greatest obstacle to peace for them is being pulled in two separate directions at the same time. Playing wishbone for the devil is to make his wish come true—you will be broken in two.

72

Recognize False Guilt

*If we confess our sins, he is faithful and just to forgive us our sins,
and to cleanse us from all unrighteousness.*

(1 John 1:9)

All sin, in order to be put away once for all, needs forgiveness. Until sin is confessed and forsaken it is bound to eat at the conscience. However, some guilt doesn't relate to sin at all. This is called *false guilt*. This type of guilt occurs when unscripturally strict rules, self-devised, get broken. For instance, a person who has decided to read two chapters of the Bible every day forgets to read one day or falls asleep after reading only one chapter. The next day guilt sets in. Is this true guilt? Definitely not! There are no biblical commands on the length of portions to read.

Human goals are good. They get us somewhere instead of nowhere. But they are not the cement of life. Feeling guilty over failing a personal preference or standard is no cause for guilt. At the same time, we should not excuse true guilt brought on by sinful behavior.

73

Reject Materialism

Do not love the world, nor the things in the world. If any one loves the world, the love of the Father is not in him. For all that is in the world, the lust of the flesh and the lust of the eyes and the boastful pride of life, is not from the Father, but is from the world.

(1 John 2:15–16, NASB)

Materialism is the widest gulf that divides many Christians from inner peace. They are absorbed in possessions and cannot rest until they have that new hot item. All priorities drop one notch to raise this latest fad to number one. Once it is secured, Satan sees to it that another takes its place. This is better known as the let's-keep-up-with-the-Joneses game.

The whole drive behind the possession lifestyle is self-image. The materialist isn't comfortable enough with self, so the old ego seeks bolstering with the nicest furnishings available. The trouble is they never satisfy.

Peace is never found in the pot at the end of the rainbow, but in the rainbow itself, whose Maker is God. Peace is finding unsearchable wealth by seeing life from his perspective.

PART SIX

Developing Strength
for Daily Living

74

Call Sin What It Is

For I confess my iniquity; I am full of anxiety because of my sin.
(Psalm 38:18, NASB)

A common trick of the old sinful nature is to excuse away sin. This is usually done by passing it off as some "lesser" evil. Other people excuse it by brashly proclaiming their wrongdoing as acceptable behavior. Still others employ another method of rationalizing: they use accommodation. By twisting Bible verses into theological knots, they attempt to justify their wrong; such justification almost borders on blasphemy.

During this little charade, sin continues doing its damage. Until it is labeled correctly, admitted, and confessed, sinful behavior will mount its powerful anxiety attack. Eventually, something snaps! Just read the psalm again.

75

Be Serious About It

He will call upon me, and I will answer him; I will be with him in trouble; I will rescue him.

(Psalm 91:15, NASB)

When we are in trouble it is wise to ask ourselves, "Do I really want to be helped?" Strangely, I have met people that have literally refused to give up their problems. Their problems are like a broken leg, they receive much attention from others by being so "needy." These individuals seldom improve and certainly not for long. They have not learned to get their needs for attention met through healthy interactions. Being needy can become a hobby. However, if we do want real help, this verse is for us. We can feel the anxiety flow out and away from us as we rest in God's faithfulness.

76

Know Your Limitations

As far as the east is from the west, so far hath he removed our transgressions from us. Like as a father pitieth his children, so the Lord pitieth them that fear him. For he knoweth our frame; he remembereth that we are dust.

(Psalm 103:12–14)

God knows that we are weak, so should we. He considers our human limitations and is empathetic toward us. But men have a corny macho ideal to live up to, and women are increasingly consumed with the equality ethic. We all drive ourselves to the brink of frenzy trying to climb the ladder of success. After getting up only a short way we realize we are afraid of heights.

There is a moral here. We are flawed and, even though God has completely forgiven us, we shouldn't invite stress into our lives by trying to live life in human strength alone. It is God who breathes into dust the breath of life. He has no limitations. Walk in his strength.

77

Don't Be a Workaholic!

It is vain that you rise up early and late to rest, eating the bread of anxious toil; for he gives to his beloved sleep.

(Psalm 127:2, RSV)

In this Bible verse is a warning: do not be too anxious or too zealous in your work. In other words, don't be a workaholic! It is self-destructive to push ourselves too hard day and night. The end result is often collapse, exhaustion, anxiety, and broken relationships with others. It is far better to work and live in moderation, avoiding extremes. If we toil, but not feverishly, God will grant us the restful sleep we need.

78

Anchor Your Thoughts

Thou dost keep him in perfect peace, whose mind is stayed on thee, because he trusts in thee.

(Isaiah 26:3, RSV)

Some people's minds are lost at sea—drifting carelessly, aimlessly on the waves of imagination. They spend too much time conjuring up problems that don't even exist and not nearly enough time zeroing in on the positive promises of God. When one comes to the ocean of God's love or the sea of his forgiveness, it would be wise to cast down an anchor. As the verse says, stay there for awhile.

79

Wait for Emotional Strength

Do you not know? Have you not heard?
The everlasting God, the LORD, the creator of
*   the ends of the earth*
Does not become weary or tired.
His understanding is inscrutable.
He gives strength to the weary,
And to him who lacks might He increases
*   power.*
Though youths grow weary and tired,
And vigorous young men stumble badly,
Yet those who wait for the Lord
Will gain new strength;
They will mount up with wings like eagles,
They will run and not get tired,
They will walk and not become weary.
                    (Isaiah 40:28–31, NASB)

When we are anxious and depressed, we become weary, we become tired. In this condition if we do not rely on the Lord we may stumble. But God never wearies or tires. He desires to give us strength and encouragement as we become more dependent on him for our emotional stability.

80

Evaluate Your Outlook

Therefore I tell you, do not be anxious about your life, what you shall eat or what you shall drink, nor about your body, what you shall put on. Is not life more than food, and the body more than clothing? Look at the birds of the air: they neither sow nor reap nor gather into barns, and yet your heavenly Father feeds them. Are you not of more value than they? And which of you by being anxious can add one cubit to his span of life? And why are you anxious about clothing? Consider the lilies of the field, how they grow; they neither toil nor spin; yet I tell you, even Solomon in all his glory was not arrayed like one of these. But if God so clothes the grass of the field, which today is alive and tomorrow is thrown into the oven, will he not much more clothe you, O men of little faith?

(Matthew 6:25–30, RSV)

Sometimes we get too wrapped up in life's details. The separate ingredients of culture and lifestyle captivate us so thoroughly that we lose our perspective on life itself. While we scurry like mice through a hedge maze, the real beauty of life lies just beyond the bushes. And what is that beauty? Simplicity.

This is the secret key that unlocks the shackles of confusion. And isn't confusion what we visualize so much of life to be? Sometimes it almost becomes a Chinese fire drill.

Notice the simple elegance of our Lord's words in this passage. He told them they had a faith problem. They tried to figure everything out. They needed a new outlook, the outlook of faith: simple, childlike faith.

81

Don't Overplan for Tomorrow!

Therefore do not be anxious for tomorrow; for tomorrow will care for itself. Each day has enough trouble of its own.

(Matthew 6:34, NASB)

In the smash-hit Broadway play, *Annie*, the lead character sings the popular song, "Tomorrow." In that song she proudly proclaims, "I love you, tomorrow, you're only a day away."

Unlike Annie, many people worry themselves to madness over tomorrow. They have staged in their minds the various possible tragedies they expect to happen. It's a case of overplanning. This borderline paranoia is responsible for the overthrow of several character traits. Naturally, peace is gone as well.

It is a mistake to look totally beyond today. Wise planning certainly isn't wrong, but fruitless worrying is! Living today to the fullest is the best way to approach tomorrow. I would suppose that, if a little orphan like Annie can get so excited about tomorrow, then surely we can find hope for our tomorrows, even if only in living through the challenges of our todays.

82

Reorient Your Priorities

But the Lord answered and said to her, "Martha, Martha, you are worried and bothered about so many things."

(Luke 10:41, NASB)

Martha had things out of whack. She had allowed her highest priority—learning from Jesus—to be replaced by busyness. The result was worry and nervousness.

How often this happens to Christians today! Priorities shift and Jesus Christ takes a back seat to lesser values! Purpose and direction are lost and anxiety gets a stranglehold on the well-meaning Marthas who are more caught up in doing than they are in growing.

Essential to the spiritual health of every believer are correct priorities. These priorities revolve around our values, the things we consider important. The person battling worry should examine priorities to be sure the Martha syndrome hasn't gotten him or her.

83

Be Victorious

I have said this to you, that in me you may have peace. In the world you have tribulation; but be of good cheer, I have overcome the world.

(John 16:33, RSV)

Christ has already won the battle; now all we have to do is claim the victory. Have you heard that before? It's true, but not quite as simple as it sounds. One does not suddenly become an overcomer by simply saying with confidence, "I am an overcomer!"

Victory begins when, through the power of Jesus Christ, we find peace in living life. When we are *absorbed* in our Lord, the fear-inspiring challenges that intimidate us can be met with "good cheer," for it is then that the Lord brings us victory in the world that he has already overcome.

84

Mature Through Adversity

And we know that God causes all things to work together for good to those who love God, to those who are called according to His purpose.

(Romans 8:28, NASB)

In the early 1970s, Holmes and Rahe developed a chart assigning "life change units" to various situational changes and problems (such as the death of a relative, illness, retirement, financial problems, job changes, and change in residence). They found that an accumulation of two hundred or more units in a single year results in a significant increase in psychiatric problems (such as anxiety).

Romans 8:28 can be a tremendous comfort to God's children when they are going through situational problems. God promises to make all of our circumstances work together for good, in the long run. This does not mean that God causes all our problems, as some Christians erroneously suppose. God may direct some of them, and we can be assured that no situation arises without God's permitting it. Moreover, no difficult circumstances will ever come our way without God being intimately involved in our lives. In every situational problem, whether God directs it or permits it, he will teach us lessons that will benefit us greatly, in the long run.

It should also be noted that Christians bring a great many problems on themselves, either consciously or subconsciously. But God will make even our self-imposed situational problems work together for good.

85

Reprogram Your Computer Brain

And do not be conformed to this world, but be transformed by the renewing of your mind, that you may prove what the will of God is, that which is good and acceptable and perfect.

(Romans 12:2, NASB)

The brain is a fascinating organ. It functions with a capacity more complex than any manmade computer. And yet, there are times when ideas need to be flushed from its system and replaced with new data. Whenever the ideology of this world circumvents the free flow of spiritual insight, then the mind must be renewed in the transforming power of God's forgiveness and cleansing. Without plugging into fresh intimacy with Christ, the mind will slowly corrode with the peace-endangering philosophies of this world.

86

Expect Some Pressure Situations

And I was with you in weakness and in much fear and trembling.
(1 Corinthians 2:3, RSV)

This whole book would lose its purpose if it attempted to say that we will never have difficult moments. We will! In this verse we can quickly see that even the apostle Paul had some bouts with fear and anxiety. But Paul remained secure in the knowledge that his faith in God's power and God's wisdom would be sufficient. As a result, he was not overpowered by his problems. The pressure only tempered him into a better servant for the Lord Jesus Christ.

87

Develop a Positive Outlook

I can do all things in him who strengthens me.
(Philippians 4:13, RSV)

There is a clear principle in the popular phrase: Never say never again! "I can't," are words counselors hear so frequently. They are the words of the lazy, the passive, the defeated, and the weary, none of whom has a positive outlook.

This verse does not say God will do everything for us, as some Christians have foolishly believed. Rather, it holds the promise that he will give us the strength we need to deal with our problems in biblical ways. With this kind of team strength, we can look positively at our circumstances, believing God will bring us through them.

88

Identify with Christ

For we have not a high priest which cannot be touched with the feeling of our infirmities; but was in all points tempted like as we are, yet without sin. Let us therefore come boldly unto the throne of grace, that we may obtain mercy, and find grace to help in time of need.

(Hebrews 4:15–16)

One tool utilized in group psychotherapy to help individuals deal with anxiety is identification with others who also have faced problems in life. It is helpful to realize that one does not stand alone, that others have withstood similar storms of life; they understand and they care.

The writer of Hebrews tells us that Christ is such a person. Christ understands our weaknesses and temptations, and invites us to tell him about them, so that he can offer grace to help in these times of need. Identify with Christ. He feels the pain you are going through. He too has felt temptation and pain, weakness, and rejection.

89

Keep Growing Spiritually

As newborn babes, desire the sincere milk of the word, that ye may grow thereby.

(1 Peter 2:2)

It is hard to believe, but some Christians often hit a plateau in their spiritual growth. Worse than that, they appear to like it that way. Their hunger for spiritual things has been overtaken by other appetites. When temptations increase, they have less and less inner strength to resist. Complicate this weakness with anxiety and the result is distressed individuals ready to accept Satan's moments of relief (through such things as alcohol, drugs, and immoral sex) in exchange for what eventually becomes months, even years, of regret.

The innocent craving of more spiritual food from God's Word, like that of an infant for milk, needs to be revived in many of the worry-riddled souls. Feeding on the Word of God brings satiating comfort and peace.

90

Loosen Your Grip

Humble yourselves therefore under the mighty hand of God, that he may exalt you in due time: Casting all your care upon him; for he careth for you.

(1 Peter 5:6–7)

Letting go of problems isn't as easy as we might think. Most of us have such a tight grip on our problems that even after prayer they plague us as much as they did before. We keep casting our cares upon the Lord, but they seem to be super-glued to our fingers. We just can't let go.

Our fierce grip usually comes from the idea that somebody has to figure out an answer. After all, problems don't just work themselves out. So, when we finish praying and are unable to see immediate visible results, we continue to worry. Sometimes our grip is so intense that we abandon prayer altogether.

We must realize that God cares about us. He will bear our worries for us. In him we have a true friend who will help. And when we cast our cares in his direction, he takes control, even if we don't feel it.

Go ahead. Pry your fingers loose. The anxiety you are grasping is worthless to you.

PART SEVEN

Focusing on Christ
for Comfort

91

Get Scriptural Direction

Thy word is a lamp to my feet and a light to my path.
(Psalm 119:105, NASB)

The anxious person fears the future and does not enjoy the present. However, by studying and meditating daily on God's Word, even the anxiety-stricken individual can find true and lasting peace. God's Word lights the way for a peaceful and calmer life.

92

Claim God's Promises

Fear thou not; for I am with thee; be not dismayed; for I am thy God: I will strengthen thee; yea, I will help thee; yea, I will uphold thee with the right hand of my righteousness.

(Isaiah 41:10)

In today's fast-paced, mobile society, there are many threats to our emotional stability. Nevertheless, this same God, who ages ago comforted and supported his children with the fact of his presence, continues today to comfort and support his children in the same way. We can find peace in claiming the wonderful promises he offers us. Claim Isaiah 41:10 today!

93

Grow Some Spiritual Roots

*Blessed is the man who trusts in the Lord, whose trust is the Lord.
He is like a tree planted by water, that sends out its roots by the
stream and does not fear when heat comes, for its leaves remain
green, and is not anxious in the year of drought, for it does not cease
to bear fruit.*

(Jeremiah 17:7–8, RSV)

Now this isn't just any ordinary old tree. It is vigorous, growing, well rooted, drought resistant, and fruit-bearing. The sun can beat down on it day in and day out, but its leaves won't brown and curl. This is one determined tree; it is going to bear fruit, no matter what.

The Bible verse says that this is how blessed is the man who trusts in the Lord. His faith is well-established and in the right person, Christ. He is going to make it through the washouts in the road of life because his "trust is in the Lord." Not his I.Q., or his denomination, but the Lord is his first and final hope. This man obviously believes that God is completely trustworthy. He is allowing God to minister to him, and he is ministering to others (which is bearing fruit).

How does this verse relate to us? Although we probably won't sprout more trust in God overnight, we can take courage from this verse. We can begin to grow in our trust in God. Fertilize trust with Bible study, prayer, and wholesome fellowship with the Christian family. Chances are that, as we grow in trust, our anxieties will decrease and our blessings will increase.

94

Find Hope in God's Design

For I know the plans that I have for you, declares the Lord, plans for welfare and not for calamity to give you a future and a hope.
(Jeremiah 29:11, NASB)

Here is a tremendous truth to focus on: God has a plan. That's easy to overlook. Especially since we can't see all of it at once. Instead, we anticipate calamity—whatever can go wrong will. This is far from what God desires for us. He wants us to feel secure about the future by trusting him to complete his design in us. Suddenly, calamity turns into "calmity."

95

Make Your Needs Known

Ask, and it shall be given to you; seek, and you shall find; knock, and it shall be opened to you.

(Matthew 7:7, NASB)

Three words: ask, seek, knock. They speak of perseverance in prayer. Of being active instead of passive. Of reaching out instead of bottling up. Of looking to Christ instead of to self. And each is accompanied by a promise: it shall be given, you shall find, it shall be opened. Bright words of hope.

Three words: doubt, confusion, worry. They speak of fear. Of discouragement and despair. Of anxiety and hopelessness. Of dwelling on the negative instead of the positive. They hold no promises. But they are curable by matching them with the first three words:

ask—doubt
seek—confusion
knock—worry

Usually, when one of the second set of words is at work, the corresponding word from the first set is not. Put your actions to the test.

96

Exchange Yokes

Come unto me, all ye that labor and are heavy laden, and I will give you rest. Take my yoke upon you, and learn of me; for I am meek and lowly in heart: and ye shall find rest unto your souls. For my yoke is easy, and my burden is light.

(Matthew 11:28–30)

Christ invites the anxious person to embark on a supernatural adventure: the adventure of learning from the Scriptures and the Holy Spirit those things that produce the internal rest that only God can give. Many Christians try to cover up their anxieties by taking on more and more work. They become workaholics to avoid looking at themselves or their true feelings. They fool themselves into thinking these additional responsibilities are from God. Then they get angry at God for giving them such a difficult yoke and such heavy burdens.

In reality, the difficult yoke and heavy burdens are not from God, but are self-imposed. They are a choice, perhaps handed down from perfectionistic, over-demanding parents or from a legalistic, negativistic church. They may even be a compensation for suppressed inferiority feelings and a fear of failure.

God wants us to cast off our self-imposed difficult tasks and heavy burdens and replace them with his easy yoke and light burden. We don't need to waste our time doing twenty superfluous chores a day to prove our worth. It is better to do every day two or three things which God convinces us to do, and to do them well! When we slow down, we will finally become aware of those repressed, subconscious feelings and motives.

Change yokes and start this adventure into peace. I dare you.

97

Intimacy

O Jerusalem, Jerusalem, thou that killest the prophets, and stonest them which are sent unto thee, how often would I have gathered thy children together, even as a hen gathereth her chickens under her wings, and ye would not!

(Matthew 23:27)

Some people don't want a close relationship with Jesus Christ. It threatens their lifestyle and their image. And yet, they want the benefits of spiritual intimacy (such as answered prayers, stronger faith, and peace). Christianity doesn't operate this way. We must meet God under his terms, instead of expecting him to meet us under ours.

Jesus wanted to gather Jerusalem under his protection, but they didn't like his conditions—repentance and forgiveness. Jerusalem wanted a Messiah, but in their opinion Jesus didn't fit the bill. He didn't measure up to their religious code. He made them feel uncomfortable with their complacency.

That is why so many reject Jesus today. A lack of peace with God is their greatest problem.

98

Be Set Free

I want you to be free from anxieties.

(1 Corinthians 7:32, RSV)

How clear this is! How obvious! God wants us to be free from anxiety. Anxiety continues because of our lack of faith to look at the truth: God wants us to be free. He wants us to have faith in him and look for the truth in ourselves, even if it is painful to do so. The truth will set us free (John 8:32): free from our anxieties.

99

Pray Specifically

Be anxious for nothing, but in everything by prayer and supplication with thanksgiving let your requests be made known to God. And the peace of God, which surpasses all comprehension, shall guard your hearts and your minds in Christ Jesus.
(Philippians 4:6–7, NASB)

Prayer is often too routine, too general, too bland, and too unreal. That is why people give up on it. They never get down to the brass tacks of prayer. Rather, they suspect that all answers from heaven hinge on the ability to sweet-talk God in just the right way.

They miss the boat altogether. Supplication—the bulls-eye of prayer—is what is most often missing. This is specific praying, completely unloading on the Lord, in plain words, the hurts and needs in one's heart. It is the pouring out of oneself to the Lord.

Break away from how's-the-weather kind of praying, and talk to God; really open up. He won't reject you or think you are foolish. He doesn't want you to impress him. Just be impressed with him!

100

Plug into the Word

For the word of God is quick, and powerful, and sharper than any two-edged sword, piercing even to the dividing asunder of soul and spirit, and of the joints and marrow, and is a discerner of the thoughts and intents of the heart.

(Hebrews 4:12)

The Word of God is quick, powerful, and sharp. It can help an individual to overcome anxiety. It can help us discern which thoughts are of God and which are not. Drinking from its myriad fountains irregularly will produce only irregular strength. How undependable! To be really prepared we must allow God's Word to do its work; we must allow it to reveal the person beneath our skin. When we honestly face our reflection in the mirror of God's truth, then the transformation is ready to begin, and peace is on the way!